cloverleaf books™

Planet Protectors

Earth Day Every Day

Lisa Bullard

illustrated by Xiao Xin

M MILLBROOK PRESS · MINNEAPOLIS

For Mom —L.B.

Millbrook Press
A division of Lerner Publishing Group, Inc.
241 First Avenue North
Minneapolis, MN 55401 U.S.A.

Website address: www.lernerbooks.com

Main body text set in Slappy Inline 18/28. Typeface provided by T26.

Library of Congress Cataloging-in-Publication Data

Bullard, Lisa.
     Earth Day every day / by Lisa Bullard ; illustrated by Xiao Xin.
       p.   cm. — (Cloverleaf books. Planet protectors)
     Includes index.
     ISBN 978–0–7613–6109–1 (lib. bdg. : alk. paper)
     1. Earth Day—Juvenile literature. 2. Environmentalism—Juvenile literature. I. Xin, Xiao, ill. II. Title.
GE195.5.B85 2012
333.72—dc22   2010053466

Manufactured in the United States of America
1 – BP – 7/15/11

The text of this book is printed on Arbor Plus paper, which is made with **30 percent recycled postconsumer waste fibers**. Using paper with postconsumer waste fibers helps to protect endangered forests, conserve mature trees, keep used paper out of landfills, save energy in the manufacturing process, and reduce greenhouse gas emissions. The remaining fiber comes from forestlands that are managed in a socially and environmentally responsible way, as certified by independent organizations. Also, the mills that manufactured this paper purchased renewable energy to cover its production.

TABLE OF CONTENTS

Chapter One

What a Mess!

My name's Trina. **I'm an Earthling.**

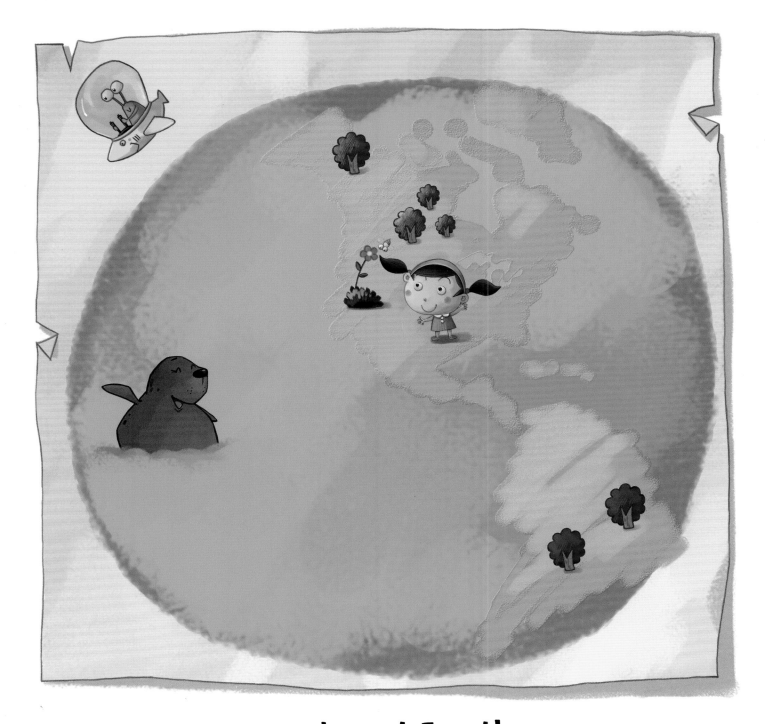

I live here on **planet Earth.** So do trees and bees and manatees. Unless you're from Mars, you're an Earthling too!

People don't always take good care of our Earth home. We do things that **hurt the Earth.**

We make the air dirty. We throw away too much. We waste power.

Mom says people should **clean up** their own **messes**.

Earthlings made this Earth mess.
So we Earthlings should fix it!

It's a job for everyone.

Chapter Two
Miss Big Mouth

My brother calls me Miss Big Mouth. So I used my big mouth to help the Earth. Last week, I asked everyone I know to plan something for **Earth Day.**

Today was finally the **big day!**

APRIL

					1	2
3	4	5	6	7	8	9
10	11	12	13	14	15	16
17	18	19	20	21	(22)	23
24	25	26	27	28	29	30

Earth Day happens once a year, on April 22. On that day, people everywhere remember to help the Earth. Earth Day also reminds us to take care of Earth all year long!

11

My teacher taught my class how to **plant trees.**

Everyone got to help. Someday our trees will grow to be much taller than we are. They'll make good homes for birds.

You can also plant special gardens to feed bees and butterflies. And trees and plants aren't just helpful to animals. They also clean the air we all breathe.

My friends formed an Earth Day club. We had our first meeting at lunch. Earth's problems mean problems for animals too. Even my favorite tigers are having trouble. So our club decided to **save money to help animals.**

Earth Day Club

$

People have
formed many groups
to help animals in trouble.
The groups find ways to protect
animals and the places they live.
They study the animals to figure out
new ways to help them. You can
learn more about these groups on
the Internet. Ask your teacher
or a parent to help
you look.

Chapter Three

My Family's Earth Day

My family and neighbors had an **Earth Day trade.**
Everybody brought stuff they don't need anymore.

It's better for the Earth when we reuse old things. *Reuse* means "to use something again." Then it doesn't end up in the trash. You also don't need to buy new things. Trading and reusing helps the Earth!

Earth Day Trade

We traded for things we want. Mom wouldn't let me trade my brother. So I traded an old puzzle for a soccer ball.

Now my family is having a special Earth night. We **turned off the TV and the computer.** That way, we don't use as much power. Instead, we're playing board games. My dog, Daisy, and I are winning!

Using power can make the air dirty. So turn off lights and machines whenever you can. Play outside instead of playing video games. Saving power helps save the Earth!

19

Maybe you can use your big mouth too? Together we can talk to everyone about **helping the Earth.** We'll ask people to make it Earth Day every day!

Then we can all find other ways to Save the Earth tomorrow.

Composting with Worms Activity

Guess what? Mom is letting me keep worms as pets!

They are a special kind of worms called redworms. They help my family compost. Composting turns certain things we throw away into something useful. The worms live in our worm compost bin. We put things like fruit and vegetable peelings in there. Eggshells go in too. That way those things don't end up in the trash.

The worms eat these things and turn them into something that looks like dirt. Don't tell my mom, but the dirt is the worm poop! The worms eat and poop a lot. Then we put the worm-made "super dirt" on our garden. Don't worry, worm poop dirt isn't stinky. It makes our plants grow strong. That's sure better than having more trash around the house. And there are lots of places you can put a worm compost bin.

Talk to your family. Or your teacher at school. Maybe you can start a worm compost bin too. Then invite some worms to lunch!

Here are two websites to help your family get started. Look for the word *vermicomposting*. That's a fancy way of saying "worm composting."

North Carolina Division of Pollution Prevention and Environmental Assistance
http://www.p2pays.org/compost/vermicomposting.asp

Wisconsin Department of Natural Resources
http://www.dnr.state.wi.us/org/caer/ce/eek/earth/recycle/wormcomp.htm

GLOSSARY

compost: to turn things like vegetable peels or leaves into something that helps plants grow

Earth Day: a special day for people around the world to help the planet

Earthling: someone who lives on planet Earth

manatee: a large, peaceful swimming animal

protect: to keep something from being hurt

reuse: to use something again

BOOKS

Boothroyd, Jennifer. *People and the Environment.* Minneapolis: Lerner Publications Company, 2008. Find out why people need a healthy Earth.

Brown, Laurie Krasny, and Marc Brown. *Dinosaurs Go Green! A Guide to Protecting Our Planet.* New York: Little, Brown, 2009. This story will help you learn more about taking care of the Earth.

O'Ryan, Ellie. *Easy to Be Green: Simple Activities You Can Do to Save the Earth.* New York: Simon & Schuster, 2009. This book is filled with activities and fun facts about helping the Earth.

WEBSITES

PBS KIDS GO!: EekoWorld
http://pbskids.org/eekoworld/index.html
This website is from PBS Kids. It has several movies that will teach you more about helping the Earth. It even has a joke-telling monkey!

Pocantico Hills School: Helpful Hints for Planet Earth
http://www.pocanticohills.org/earthday/earthday.htm
Students close to your age made an Earth Day book for you to read. They share their hopes for the Earth. There are also games to play.

Zot the Frog's NBII Kids
http://kids.nbii.gov/index.html
This website is from the U.S. Geological Survey. It has activities and stories to help you learn more about the Earth. It also tells you how to plant a tree.